Original title:
A Journey with Sea Turtles

Copyright © 2025 Creative Arts Management OÜ
All rights reserved.

Author: Theodore Sinclair
ISBN HARDBACK: 978-1-80587-243-6
ISBN PAPERBACK: 978-1-80587-713-4

Beneath the Weaving Tides

With flippers wide, they paddle slow,
In ocean's dance, they steal the show.
A turtle trip, they make it known,
With seaweed hats and shells they own.

They surf the waves, it's quite a sight,
In silly squads, they take to flight.
A jellyfish is now their foe,
But dodge they do, with quite a flow.

Enchanted Passages

They wander far in underwater realms,
With crusty pals who take the helm.
Each coral house has quite the flair,
They knock on doors, but none are there.

They giggle deep in the seaweed beds,
Trading tales with clever spreads.
One lost a shoe to an eager fish,
"Next time, I'll wear a boot!" they wish.

The Timeless Wander

In twilight's glow, they weave and glide,
With starfish jokes, they form a tribe.
Their shells are thick, but hearts are light,
Each wave is met with pure delight.

Across the sand, they waddle wide,
With crustaceans on the side.
"Oh look, a pizza!" one turtle cries,
And soon all are looking at the skies.

Celestial Shells

Under moonlit hues, they roam and play,
Chasing bubbles, with naught to say.
A flotilla far in moonbeams cast,
A turtle race is on at last!

With every flip, a splash and cheer,
They laugh at crabs, who then disappear.
What's that they see? A fish in socks!
"Is this a joke?" Oh, how it rocks!

Guardians of the Blue Expanse

In the ocean wide, they glide and sway,
With shells so shiny, they dance all day.
Floating like boats, they take their chance,
While seagulls squawk, they start to prance.

With sand on their backs and smiles so bright,
They flip and they flop, what a silly sight!
A turtle gang, oh what a crew,
They race with the fish, and the tide, too!

Where the Sea Meets the Sky

Under the sun, they bask and dream,
Waves tickle toes, and seafoam gleams.
With a jellyfish hat, they strut with flair,
Who knew fashion lived down there?

As crabs do the crabwalk, they join the band,
Tap dancing turtles, it's all unplanned!
With goggles on, they dive to spy,
At the clownfish' dance, oh my, oh my!

Echoing the Depths' Ancient Call

Bubbles rise up as they chatter and cheer,
Climbing seaweed, they have no fear.
A turtle with style, flippers in sync,
At the kelp disco, they'll make you wink!

They sing to the whales, a whimsical tune,
Under the light of a glowing moon.
With quirky moves in their ocean parade,
Turtle tales under the sea are made!

Beneath the Lighthouse Glow

At night they gather, all shells aglow,
Telling tall tales 'bout sharks, don't you know?
With laughs shared among the fishy crowd,
Making waves in the dark, they're feeling proud.

One turtle said, 'Let's paint the town!'
And off they went with their paintbrush crown.
Colors splash like confetti what a scene,
Under the lighthouse, the ocean shines clean!

Echoes of the Sea

Underwater disco, turtles dance,
They wiggle and giggle, in a playful trance.
With shells like hats, they spin and sway,
Waving at fish, in their funky parade.

Bubbles pop loudly, a laugh in the blue,
As jellyfish join in, with a jig or two.
They flip and they flop, all in good fun,
The ocean's a party, and it's just begun.

Circles in the Sand

Turtles in the sand, having a blast,
Digging up treasures from the sea's vast past.
Playing in circles, they trace funny lines,
Making sandcastles that look like porcupines.

The waves crash in, but they don't seem to care,
Rolling about without a single fare.
With seashells as crowns, they strut on the shore,
Laughing together, what's life's not for?

Sailors of the Deep

Sailors aboard, those turtles so spry,
Navigating currents, oh me, oh my!
With a map made of seaweed, they set their course,
Following bubbles, a natural source.

They chat with the crabs, all ready to trade,
For bits of sea glass, a jeweled cascade.
Their stories are wild, with humor so bright,
Sailing through kelp forests, what a delight!

Oceanic Odyssey

In the great wide blue, turtles take flight,
With goggles and flippers, oh what a sight!
They glide like the wind, with giggles galore,
Playing hide and seek, with a clam at the door.

They wear ocean hats, made of coral and sea,
Inviting the dolphins for some coffee.
With every splash, they burst into song,
An oceanic tale where they all belong.

Coral Kingdoms

In a realm of coral bright,
Turtles dance with pure delight.
They wiggle, jiggle, take a spin,
Then giggle at the fish within.

Flippers flapping, what a sight!
Dodging crabs that scuttle tight.
With every twist and silly turn,
They laugh out loud, the tides they churn.

The Wanderers Below

Beneath the waves they roam and play,
A bunch of turtles heading away.
One lost his map, the other just pranks,
They end up crashing into the tanks!

With goofy grins and shells so wide,
They slide and glide at fishy tide.
Sardines cackle, saying, "Hey!"
As turtles tango, come what may!

Secrets of the Current

Secrets whisper in the brine,
Turtles plotting all the time.
"What's the deal with seaweed hats?"
"Fashion statement!" says the brats.

Riding currents, like a breeze,
They chase each other with great ease.
A sneaky dolphin joins the fray,
"I bet you can't catch me today!"

Swimmers in the Sun

Under sun, they bask and glide,
Turtle pals side by side.
One lost his snack to a seagull bold,
"Hey, bring that back! I'm not that old!"

With laughter bright, they float around,
Playing hide and seek, truly unbound.
A flip, a splash, a playful quack,
Their sunny antics never lack.

Remnants of the Past

In the surf they glide with grace,
Carrying shells in a funny race.
With goggles on, they play peek-a-boo,
As waves wash secrets just for a few.

Sandy tales of salty glee,
They laugh at fishy history.
Each bubble is a story told,
Of daring days and nights so bold.

Whirling Waters

Round and round in currents they spin,
Chasing crabs, let the fun begin!
With flippers flapping, they twirl and dive,
Feeling like stars in a sea-weed jive.

With a wink of an eye, they dash past the fleet,
A turtle conga, oh, what a treat!
In whirlpools deep, they spin like tops,
Who knew the ocean had such fun hops?

The Longing for Home

Under the moon, they paddle in dreams,
Plotting the path of seaweed streams.
With a giggle, they drift along,
High-fiving dolphins, singing a song.

But just a glance at the beachy shore,
Makes them wonder what's waiting in store.
A hammock made of sea grass invites,
To nap in sunlight, oh what delights!

Mosaic of the Ocean Floor

Colorful tiles of sea shells galore,
Turtles play checkers on the ocean floor.
With seahorse friends, they set the scene,
A living room made of marine cuisine.

Crabs complain, 'This game's so unfair!'
As turtles chuckle and shake the water's hair.
Each treasure they find a wondrous delight,
Making memories that sparkle so bright!

The Current's Secret Keepers

Underwater capers, they glide with cheer,
Silly sea turtle races, the ocean's gears.
Flipping their flippers, they dance in the waves,
Laughing with fishes, they're the ocean's knaves.

A turtle named Ted tried to ride a fish,
Swam in circles, oh what a silly wish!
With a splash and a squeal, he plopped down low,
Yelled to his buddy, "Did you see that show?"

Charting the Celestial Shores

At dusk they gather, shells aglow,
Planning their escapade, high or low.
Under the stars, with giggles and grins,
They flipmapped the beach for the best of spins.

One turtle claimed to know the way,
Pulled out a map made of seaweed play.
"To the best kelp draws!" he waved it through,
But got lost in laughter, not knowing what's true!

Tales from the Briny Depths

A turtle named Lulu told a wild tale,
Of a clam who danced in a jellyfish veil.
"He jiggled and wiggled, the crowd in a trance,
But tripped on a sea sponge, lost in his dance!"

Then Carl just chuckled, said it was fake,
"Clams can't dance, for goodness' sake!"
But the bubbles kept rising, the laughter grew loud,
As they shared other tales of their ocean crowd.

Shells and Stars in the Moonlight

Under a full moon, they gathered in fun,
Turtle talent show; oh, look at them run!
With moonlit shells sparkling, they shone like stars,
Performing their acts, strumming seaweed guitars.

A turtle named Rita recited a rhyme,
About a shrimp who thought he could fly for a time.
With a leap and a flop, he fell in the sand,
"Next year, I'll stick to the sea, yes – that's the plan!"

Legends in the Foam

Once I met a turtle bold,
With a tale of seaweed gold.
He claimed he danced with dolphins bright,
But tripped on fins in mid-flight.

He surfed the waves like a pro,
But forgot where to go, oh no!
With a grin, he'd spin and glide,
Chasing jellyfish for a ride.

In the reef, he found his crew,
With a snail that sang, oh so new.
They'd race the crabs and leap so high,
While seagulls laughed and flew by.

So next you swim, look around,
For the turtle spreading joy unbound.
With each wave, he shares his cheer,
Making sea life brighter here!

Forever Flowing

In a world where tides are tossed,
A turtle asked, 'What's the cost?
For every wave that's come and gone,
Is there a place where I belong?'

He waddled round with great delight,
Chasing fish that swam in sight.
Each splash a giggle, each dive a laugh,
He'd steal the show like a crafty calf!

"Oh look," he said, "there's a crab in a suit,
Wanna join us for a fruity loot?
We'll feast on snacks and dance till dawn,
No worries when the tide is drawn!"

They partied hard till the stars shone bright,
With seaweed confetti, what a sight!
So listen well, when by the sea,
Fun is waiting just for thee!

Guardians of the Reef

Three turtles donned their superhero capes,
Guarding reefs, like grand escape tapes.
But one forgot to take his flight,
And hugged a rock all through the night.

They saved the fish from tangled net,
Yet one turtle said, "I'm not done yet!"
He tangled up in a seaweed maze,
Creating ruckus for days and days.

While crabs would cheer them on with glee,
One turtle claimed, "Look, I'm a tree!"
With sea cucumbers as his crew,
They'd orchestrate their own sea zoo.

So next time you walk on the sand,
Think of turtles taking a stand.
For laughter lingers with every wave,
Guardians of joy, so bold and brave.

The Painted Shell

A turtle had a painted shell,
That sparkled bright like a bell.
He'd flaunt it round with laughs and cheers,
Pretending to hide from silly fears.

With polka dots and stripes galore,
He'd slip and slide on ocean floor.
"Hey, look at me!", he'd cry with glee,
"I'm the best-dressed of the sea!"

But when a wave came crashing in,
He flopped and flailed, oh what a spin!
His shell flew high, a twisty tale,
Landing at the feet of a friendly whale.

"Not so fast, my finned friend here,
Your style does bring us all the cheer!"
Together they laughed, a merry pair,
A painted shell beyond compare!

Currents of Connection

In the sun, the turtles glide,
With flip-flops on, they take the tide.
One wears shades, a stylish flair,
While another's caught in seaweed hair.

They race the waves, with goofy grins,
Playing tag with other fins.
A crab joins in, with sideways cheer,
As laughter bubbles, bright and clear.

Beneath the surface, they play hide and seek,
Turtle tags a fish, what a cheek!
A splash here, a giggle there,
In this sea, joy fills the air.

With every flip, a tale they weave,
The ocean's heart makes us believe.
In their dance, we find delight,
Waving bye to the fading light.

Under Currents of Grace

In the blue, they swirl and twirl,
We're lucky guests in their world.
With shells like armor, oh-so-bright,
They flip and flop, what a sight!

One turtle thinks it's quite the show,
Strikes a pose, puts on a flow.
He trips on sand, but giggles rise,
All while rolling his big fish eyes.

Under waves, they chat with fish,
Sharing dreams, a splashy wish.
"Swim faster!" yells one, then slips,
A bubble-trap for stylish flips!

Together they ride each crest and swell,
In a dance that no one can quell.
With every wave that pulls and gives,
They teach us all how joy really lives.

The Sky Beneath

In the calm, a turtle drops,
Wonders if the fish wear tops.
Peeking down at shapes below,
"Oh! Is that a clam in tow?"

With a wink, he startles squids,
Who swim away like nervous kids.
One turtle scoffs, and plays the fool,
"Come back, friends! We're in a school!"

The sun reflects on waves so blue,
As turtles spin in skies anew.
"Look at me! I'm flying high!"
As a jellyfish floats by with a sigh.

A twist and turn, still on the chase,
Who knew sea life could keep such pace?
With each adventure, laughter swells,
In the depths, where funny stories dwell.

Tidal Moments

A turtle hums a catchy tune,
Under the bright and shining moon.
He challenges waves to a dance-off,
As crabs clap along, all scoff!

One turtle trips and does a flip,
Invites the others for a dip.
"Catch me if you can, my friends!"
But the jellyroll laugh never ends.

As tides change, they ride the flow,
Chasing bubbles, putting on a show.
But oh, the sight! How someone slipped,
And straight into a clam, all whipped!

But laughter rains as they regroup,
Wobbling in their funny troop.
In tidal moments, life's a blast,
With every wave, they revel and last!

Driftwood and Seafoam Stories

On driftwood logs, we take our seats,
While critters dance on wobbly feet.
The seaweed wiggles, the shells all cheer,
As turtles bob about without a fear.

Bubbles burst like laugh tracks loud,
While fish form a swirling, giggling crowd.
With flippers flapping in hilarious style,
They chase jellyfish, and we can't help but smile.

A crab wears a hat, tilts to one side,
The sea turtles chuckle, full of pride.
With every splish and every splash,
Their antics leave us all in a laugh.

From sandy shores to ocean's depth,
Each flop and flip is filled with jest.
With every wave, their stories grow,
As driftwood sways and seafoam glows.

Whispers of the Tide

The tide rolls in with a cheeky grin,
While turtles tease with a silly spin.
They peek from rocks, in shells they hide,
Whispers of laughter float with the tide.

A turtle trips, it's quite a sight,
Flippers flailing, oh what a fright!
Sea urchins giggle, clams clap along,
As bubbles rise, they burst into song.

Octopuses ponder with wiggly arms,
While turtles flip, with their goofy charms.
Stinging jellyfish sing out a tune,
As turtles twirl beneath the glowing moon.

From the depths to the shore, they'll glide with glee,
Echoes of joy stretch far out to sea.
With each splash and laugh, they cultivate fun,
In the waters where mischief has begun.

Beneath the Ocean's Embrace

Beneath the waves, where the silliness flows,
The turtles gather to trade their prose.
With seaweed ties and coral crowns,
They jest and chuckle, swirling around.

A dolphin's joke, a playful tease,
The turtles roll with the greatest ease.
With this shell and that flip, they spin with delight,
Creating a scene that's a comical sight.

Shells clap together, forming a band,
While turtles boogie, wiggling on sand.
With crabs doing the cha-cha on the rocks,
They all gather 'round to share some knocks.

From the oceanic depths, a giggling sound,
A symphony of chuckles beneath the ground.
As waves crash and tummies ache from the fun,
The laughter of turtles can't be outdone.

Guardians of the Coral

With coral crowns and playful grins,
The turtles have joined in the coral spins.
They stand guard over treasures that twinkle and glow,
In their silly swim, just putting on a show.

A sea star whispers, 'Let's play hide and seek,'
The turtles comply, with a playful squeak.
Hiding behind rocks, with a glance to the side,
Oh how they giggle, in coral they abide.

The clowns of the sea, with flippers and fins,
They chase after bubbles, oh where to begin?
With starfish cheering, their laughs are all free,
Echos of joy flow through the blue sea.

Under the glitter of sunlight's embrace,
They guard their domain full of humor and grace.
The guardians of coral, with chuckles they reign,
In a world where laughter is never in vain.

Confluence of Currents

In the dance of the waves, they twirl and glide,
Sea turtles laughing, with shells open wide.
They wear silly hats as they swim side by side,
Cracking up fish, oh what a joyful ride!

With fins flapping like they're at a grand ball,
They bump into crabs, who shout, "Not at all!"
A parade of the playful, they swim and enthrall,
As seagulls cackle, making quite the raucous call!

They bump and they tumble, not worried a beat,
Chasing the bubbles that float like a treat.
Each turtle a jester, in their silly fleet,
Making the ocean their comedic retreat!

And when night falls, they still can't relax,
They'll play hide and seek with some lurking flacks.
In this watery world, laughter never lacks,
With a splash and a giggle, they're back on their tracks!

Pathway of the Shell-Backed

Strolling along with their shells on their backs,
Our funny friends share their goofiest hacks.
"If you see a wave, just get up and relax!"
"Pretend it's a trampoline, and do some high-tacks!"

In one swift motion, a turtle did flip,
Landed in kelp, and let out a quip.
"Oh dear, I'm stuck! I need a good grip!"
As his pals all tumbled and doubled in zip!

Through coral gardens, they wander and play,
Turning every rock into a cabaret stage.
With performers and jesters, it's quite the display,
"Who's ready for dance-offs?" they all yell with glee!

With a wobble and splash, they steer through the blue,
Telling tales of the snacks that they got to pursue.
A buffet of jelly and seaweed to chew,
"Who's hungry? No worries, there's plenty for you!"

Heartbeats of the Ocean

In the pulse of the tide, a giggle's heart beats,
With turtles tumbling, striking odd poses in fleets.
"Look at me go!" shouts a turtle who sneaks,
While trying to moonwalk on slippery sheets!

They race with the dolphins, a comical show,
"I'll beat you with style! Just wait and then go!"
Fins flapping wildly, while laughter does flow,
As the waves echo joy, putting on quite the flow!

And in the sea's orchestra, bubbles do pop,
Each splash a new tune, the whole ocean's hip-hop.
The turtles are jesters, and they just can't stop,
With a flip and a twist, they dance all on top!

At sunset's embrace, they gather and cheer,
For every fun moment, they hold oh so dear.
With a wink and a nod, they all persevere,
In this goofy ballet, there's nothing to fear!

Murmurs of the Salty Deep

In whispers of tides, the turtles conspire,
To tell of the mishaps that lift spirits higher.
"Remember last week when I got caught in the wire?"
"Yeah! You looked like a noodle!" - The laughter's desire!

Swirling in circles, they plot their next prank,
The fish look confused, but they just laugh and flank.
"Let's tickle a shark!" one turtle gave thanks,
While another refused, "That'll cause a real crank!"

They dive into bubbles, creating a blend,
A funny adventure with twist and a bend.
One turtle breaks out with a floppy rear end,
As his pals can't contain it, they shiver and send!

With the moonlight above, they giggle and play,
Murmurs of joy spread, like foam in the spray.
These turtle comedians brighten the day,
With shells full of laughter, come join in the fray!

Guardians of the Deep

In shells like armor, they swim with glee,
Guardians of secrets beneath the sea.
With flippers so flappy, they dance and glide,
Making fish giggle as they take a ride.

They've got no worries, no clocks, no cares,
Just munching on seaweed, and cracking some stares.
Their laughter echoes through coral aligned,
While dolphins all cheer, 'You're one of a kind!'

As they chase after bubbles, oh what a sight,
They twirl and they swirl, all day and all night.
With a wink and a nod, they're off on a spree,
The ocean their playground—come join them, whee!

So let's raise a toast with our kelp-filled mugs,
Here's to the turtles who give us the hugs.
With fun in the currents and joy on the flow,
They're the life of the party—come on, let's go!

Navigator of Dreams

In the moonlight's shimmer, they plot their course,
Navigators wise, with a giggle, of course.
They hitch a ride on a jellyfish float,
While joking with seahorses, they gleefully gloat.

Plotting stars hidden in waters so deep,
A map made of laughter ensures they'll not weep.
With turtle-sized compasses made from a shell,
They'll find all the wonders where sea critters dwell.

From reefs to the currents, they frolic and roam,
The ocean's their highway, their home sweet home.
With a splash and a twirl, they break through the waves,
Showing us all how the wild world behaves.

So grab your flippers and join in the fun,
With turtles, the dreamers, the race has begun!
By starlight they wander, in laughter they beam,
Together we float through this magical dream.

Symphony of the Below

In oceans so blue, a concert unfolds,
Turtles are maestros, their tales never told.
With bubble-filled giggles, they play their accord,
While seaweed sways softly, a natural chord.

Each flap of their fins strikes a whimsical beat,
As crabs clap their claws, giving rhythms a seat.
Stars in the sea wink, at the show so divine,
While fishes dance wildly, in formation, in line.

A saxophone shrimp plays a sweet little tune,
And turtles hum softly beneath the fat moon.
With sea turtles leading this merry parade,
The symphony rolls on, in joy it's displayed.

So dive in with laughter, let troubles all flee,
Join the underwater revelry, can't you see?
A world of sound, fun, and magical flow,
The symphony thrives, as all creatures glow!

Elemental Trajectory

On the winds of the ocean, they laugh and they soar,
Turtles on currents, forever explore.
With shells painted bright, like a summer's delight,
They glide through the waters, oh what a sight!

Elemental wanderers, they frolic with flair,
Surfing the tides without a single care.
With sprinkles of sunlight and bubbles to chase,
They bob through the waves in this joyous space.

A dance with the seaweed, a twist with the tide,
These turtles are silly, and oh, how they glide!
With nature as stage, every tide has a twist,
They invite you to join in their humorous mist.

So follow the laughter, let worries all cease,
With turtles as friends, you'll discover your peace.
With antics aplenty and smiles that won't fade,
In the currents of fun, a grand adventure is made!

Rhythms of the Reef Choreographers

In the depths where the green ones glide,
They wiggle and twist with a joyful pride.
Their flippers are fans, in a dance so spry,
Who knew sea turtles were born to fly?

They crash into coral in countless pirouettes,
Bumping into fish who threw fishing nets.
With jellyfish parties, oh what a ball!
They two-step with rays, and everyone's tall!

Their shells hold secrets, but they won't share the loot,
For every old turtle has a well-rehearsed scoot.
With laughter in bubbles, they glide through the spray,
Making the ocean their stage every day.

So join in their waltz when you swim on through,
And try not to laugh, it's the least you could do!
For the rhythms of reef are a sight to behold,
With turtles who groove, oh, the stories they've told!

The Long Path to the Horizon

On a leisurely stroll with a very short stride,
A turtle named Timmy took off with some pride.
With a hat made of kelp and a grin like a fool,
He claimed he was off to a far distant school.

The waves tickled Timmy, who wasn't too bright,
He thought it was land, but it felt like a kite.
As seagulls chuckled, he tiptoed along,
He twirled and he spun, serenaded by song.

"Hey, buddy," said Frank, a fish passing by,
"Whatever you're chasing, it's *way* in the sky!"
But Timmy just winked, kept his focus so grand,
With dreams of a finish line drawn in the sand.

After hours of swimming, he flopped on the beach,
"I've made it!" he panted, "Success now within reach."
But there wasn't a school or a trophy in sight,
Just a few human kids, laughing with delight!

Ocean's Slowest Voyage

Oh, the ocean's quite vast, and the currents are fast,
But Terry the turtle took it in his grasp.
With a chill in his shell and a yawning so wide,
His pace was so lazy, boat races defied.

"Wave after wave," Terry sighed with good cheer,
"Who cares about rushing? The snacks will come near!"
His friends zoomed past, in a whirlwind they flew,
While he settled down for a nap by the blue.

He dreamed of fine kelp and a banquet of shells,
As fish drove by in their shimmering swells.
"You kids are too fast, you'll miss all the fun!"
Said Terry the turtle, still bathing in sun.

Eventually reaching the coral buffet,
He feasted on goodies, all carefree and gay.
So slow and so steady, he won in his way,
While others just zoomed past, in a frantic ballet!

Starlit Passages Underwater

At night when the ocean turned all sparkly blue,
The turtles decided to hold a grand queue.
With starlight above them, they summoned a dance,
Each move like a wave, oh, they took a chance!

They paddled like crazy with moonlight as guide,
Their shells twinkling bright, oh, they took quite the ride.
"Hey, Larry the lobster, come join in our fun!
We'll shimmy like seahorses 'til morning's begun!"

The crabs clapped their claws in a rhythmic spree,
As turtles spun dizzy, just living carefree.
With laughter like ripples that echoed around,
They danced in the glow where pure joy could be found.

And when dawn broke softly, their party grew pale,
They floated back home, with a soft exhale.
They whispered, "Dear sea, let the starlight return,
For tonight we shall dance — oh, so much to learn!"

Under the Waves of Wisdom

In a field of seaweed, they dance and spin,
With flippers flapping, they grin a big grin.
Eating jelly donuts, they hold them tight,
A feast of sweet jelly, what a silly sight!

They race with the current, oh what a show,
With friends by their side, they put on a glow.
A turtle named Larry, so clever and slick,
Taught others to dance, and they picked up the trick!

One turtle in shades said, 'Life's just a breeze!'
While munching on kelp, they laughed with such ease.
With bubbles attached, they zoomed through the blue,
Who knew that a turtle could laugh like a fool!

As they floated around in a sea full of cheer,
They shared turtle stories, at least a dozen a year.
With corny old jokes and a splash of their tails,
They spun woven tales, with giggles and gales.

Echoes of the Ocean's Guardians

Beneath the bright waves, in a turtle parade,
Each one was a star, with a bright shell displayed.
'Hey, don't swim too fast!' yelled a turtle named Gary,
'I'll lose my cool shades, and that would be scary!'

A sea turtle band was playing a tune,
Puffing up bubbles, they danced with the moon.
'Watch out for the crab!' chattered young Benny,
'He won't share his popcorn, not even a penny!'

With laughter and joy echoing wide,
The turtles swam on, with their pure green pride.
'Guess who's got moves?' shouted sassy Sue,
'With flippers like mine, I could start a sea zoo!'

With starfish as friends, they twirled and they spun,
Life's better together—more turtles, more fun!
They toasted with clams, in deep ocean's embrace,
Surely, each day is a silly wild race!

Beneath the Shells of Time

Beneath ancient waves, turtles wiggle and squirm,
With shells that tell stories, they share every term.
They say, 'Once we were newbies, oh what a time,
With awkward little flips, our moves in their prime!'

Old grandpa turtle yawned from the sand,
'I ate a sea sponge that tasted so bland.
But now I munch on the finest of goods,
Tasting kelp tacos in peaceful sea woods!'

When a turtle gets tired, they take a long break,
Letting the waves rock them, it's all in good sake.
They dream of the days, with their young ones in sight,
Of synchronized swimming—what a silly delight!

Time drifts like the currents, their smiles won't fade,
For these ocean jesters, life's a grand parade.
With laughter and love, beneath fickle mists,
They glide through the waters, and share gentle twists.

Glide Through the Tides

In the currents of laughter, turtles glide with ease,
Each wave tells a joke, carried softly by the breeze.
'Watch out for the whales, they'll steal all our snacks!'
Squealed speedy Sandy, as she huddled in packs.

They flip through the foam, with a splash and a dive,
Every turtle smiles, feeling so very alive.
With a tap dance on shells like a silly tap show,
They leap from the depths, going high, then below!

From coral to caves, they roam far and wide,
Wearing hats made of seaweed, with laughter, they glide.
A party of turtles, in a festival bright,
Dancing to tunes that echoed at night!

So here's to the turtles, let's raise up a cheer,
For their jests and their laughs, spreading love far and near.
With bubbles of giggles, they light up the sea,
Every wave is a story, come join, don't you see?

Stories of the Blue Realm

In the splashy waves, they take a dive,
With goofy grins, they really thrive.
Their shells, all shiny, like fancy cars,
Dancing in currents, beneath the stars.

A jellyfish jokes, 'Hey, want a ride?'
But those turtles just giggle, filled with pride.
They flip and flop, in an ocean ballet,
While seaweed's their hat, on this silly day.

Chasing the bubbles, like children at play,
They waddle on sand, and twirl all day.
Enchants the fish, with their wacky charms,
As they prance about, causing sea alarms!

When sunset arrives, they gather around,
With tales of the sea, that's football profound.
Each turtle tells stories, of all their fun,
With laughter and joy, till the day is done.

Chasing Sunbeams on Water

Flippers flapping, they leap with glee,
Chasing sunbeams, wild and free.
One turtle stumbles, lands on its back,
And yells, 'Help, I'm lost on this sunny track!'

Salty sea breeze and silly grins,
Frolicking friends, where the laughter begins.
They roll in the waves, like fish out of school,
While crabs look on, thinking, 'What a fool!'

A friendly dolphin joins in the race,
Making silly faces, full of grace.
Turtles swim faster, showing their might,
As they splash around, from day until night.

With a flip and a flop, they gather their crew,
Painting the sea with colors so blue.
Each sunset a canvas, their joy all aglow,
In the dance of the tides, they put on a show!

Treasures Beneath the Foam

Beneath the waves, they twirl and glide,
With flippers wide, they're full of pride.
Eating jelly that wobbles just right,
They dance through bubbles, oh what a sight!

With goofy faces, they roam the sea,
While asking the fish, "What's for tea?"
They wear shells like a fashion parade,
Donning seaweed hats that never quite fade.

Sometimes they stumble, not quite so keen,
While riding a wave, they're quite the scene!
With comical stunts, they flop and plop,
These ocean goofballs just can't seem to stop.

At sunset's cue, they gather 'round,
Telling jokes while the sun goes down.
With flippers waving, they spark a laugh,
Creating joy in the ocean's half!

Guardians of the Green

In seas of emerald, they rule the land,
With shells like shields, oh isn't it grand?
They giggle with crabs who pinch and tease,
As they frolic and dance in the gentle breeze.

These quirky knights in the aquatic show,
Guardians of gardens where the kelp can grow!
They take a break, munching on treats,
Laughing at leaping and twirling sea beats.

With a wink to the starfish upon the shore,
They joke about shells and wave with a roar!
In a world of water, they find their groove,
With silly antics that make you move!

When darkness falls, under stars they play,
Sharing tales of the silliest day.
With a flip and a flap, they snuggle tight,
Guardians of green, both silly and bright!

Wayfarers of the Waves

On a surf of laughter, they set their sail,
With a splash and a flip, they tell a tale.
Spreading joy like sea foam leaves,
They glide near shores with all their heaves.

The ocean's the stage, they're the stars of the show,
Wiggling their tails with a whole lot of glow!
Each wave brings a giggle, a quirk, and a flip,
As friends bumper-car in a turtle-shaped ship.

With barnacles stuck on their shell-hatted heads,
They laugh at the dolphins while shunning their beds.
In sandy salons for sunbathing fun,
They lay side by side, shining bright like the sun.

When wandering waves come crashing in,
These travelers of tides just laugh and spin.
With whimsical tales of their ocean spree,
Wayfarers of waves, forever carefree!

Echoing Lullabies

In the hush of the tide, they softly hum,
Sharing lullabies, a rhythmic strum.
With grannies of seaweed, their voices rise,
Creating a symphony beneath the skies.

Sneaky little fish join in the fun,
Wiggling and giggling, oh how they run!
As turtles chuckle through waters so deep,
They rock tiny crabs into a sweet sleep.

With wise old turtles spinning tales of yore,
Whispering secrets from ocean's core.
Echoes of laughter blend with the breeze,
Painting the ocean with memories that please.

So when you hear waves, rocking and free,
Remember the turtles, and their melody.
With hearts full of humor and joy on the rise,
Echoing lullabies, beneath twinkling skies!

Silent Navigators of the Deep

In the ocean blue, they glide and sway,
With shells they wear, they dance all day.
Flippers flapping, what a sight!
Underwater disco, oh what delight!

They dodge the fish and surf the waves,
With silly grins, they misbehave.
Finding snacks among the reeds,
Their chilly snacks are not for deeds!

They play with bubbles, blow them high,
Chasing currents like they could fly.
Weightless whispers, a watery jest,
These critters know how to enjoy the fest!

In schools of fish, they twirl, they leap,
Making friends where the sea is deep.
A turtle's laugh—who would have guessed?
Silent navigators, their roles are the best!

Turtles in Twilight's Embrace

As sun dips low, they rise with cheer,
Waving goodbye to another day here.
Shells shining bright, they're such a sight,
Playing tag in the dimming light.

With yawns and stretches, they take a break,
Hatchlings giggle, full of cake.
In twilight's glow, they spin and twirl,
These turtles know how to whirl.

A party on the sand, what's the plan?
To have a feast, oh what a jam!
Munching seaweed, they feast like kings,
Eating dinner while dancing with flings!

Then off they go to find their beds,
Cuddled up with soft sea threads.
Snoring softly, dreaming of fun,
Tomorrow's pranks will have just begun!

Whispers of the Coral Highway

On the coral reef, they roll and slide,
In secret parlors, they take pride.
Whispers flow between the fins,
Turtle tales of epic wins!

With colorful fish, they share their dreams,
Playing hide and seek in sunlit beams.
Underwater gags, a funny scene,
These sea folks know how to be keen!

Sneaking past, they chuckle and wink,
Finding shells, a treasure link.
Racing seahorses and dodging rays,
These giddy turtles spend their days.

As stars come out, the sea life glows,
With glowing friends, how the laughter flows!
A chatty crew in the night so deep,
Coral highways, secrets to keep!

A Dance with the Gentle Giants

With big ol' shells and goofy grins,
They twirl and spin like ocean kings.
Slipping through waves with such a flair,
These gentle giants beyond compare.

"Watch my moves!" they call with glee,
"Can you spin just like me?"
Belly flops and playful dives,
Their dance creates happy jives.

Floating along in the moonlit sea,
Adding rhythm to the water's spree.
Their silly jives make schools frolic,
Such playful fun, just like a frolic!

At dawn they rest, their dancing done,
Dreaming of waves and the morning fun.
These gentle giants, bold and free,
Bring laughter to the deep blue spree!

Breezes and Waves of Freedom

On the beach, we found a crew,
Shells and flippers, what to do?
With our buddies, we'll take a ride,
Wobbling left, then bumping wide.

Chasing crabs and dodging nets,
Dodging lunch, we're not your pets!
A splash here, a spin and twirl,
We're the quirkiest of the whirl!

Underwater, our antics shine,
Playing tag, we feel divine.
Fishy friends all gather near,
Chuckling loud, we serenade cheer!

As the sun dips low and fades,
We giggle through the swaying glades.
With belly laughs, we sing and play,
Life's a beach—hip-hip-hooray!

Melodies of the Marine Wanderers

In the ocean, where we roam,
Turtle tunes are far from home.
Plucking seaweed, strumming pearls,
We're the jammers of the swirls!

With a wink and a funny glide,
We shimmy past the ocean's tide.
Our harmonies, a splashy jive,
Making waves, we dance alive!

We dip and dive, a motley crew,
With every quirk, we break anew.
Giggling in our flippers tight,
Serenading fish, what a sight!

Each crab and starfish sings along,
To our seaweed-busking song.
Underwater raves, we're so spry,
Making melodies as we fly!

The Endless Blue Thread

In the deep, we stitched a dream,
Tangled in the ocean's seam.
Flippers flapping, giggles loud,
Every turtle feels so proud!

Winding round the sandy bay,
We create our own ballet.
With a wiggle and a strut,
We tie knots in our own rut!

The current pulls, but we won't tire,
Chasing bubbles, fuel for fire.
Every twist, a new delight,
Sending waves of joy in flight!

As the stars come out to play,
We weave wishes to the fray.
Under the moonlit, dreamy spread,
We're the yarn of joy instead!

Navigating Dreams and Seas

With a compass made of shells,
We set off with giggles and yells.
Turtle tales of far-off lands,
Drifting 'round with silly plans!

Charting maps with seaweed ink,
Navigating thoughts, we think!
Our boat is just a rock and foam,
On this sea, we find our home.

Every wave, a twisty ride,
Swirling songs, we laugh collide.
Under clouds, we poke and tease,
Splashing friends with silly ease!

When the thunder rumbles loud,
We flutter 'neath the nature's shroud.
Through the storms, we proudly sail,
With humor as our mighty sail!

Shells of Time

Rolling on the sandy shore,
A turtle drops its snack galore.
A seagull steals a piece to eat,
While turtles roll with flippers fleet.

Time drifts by in a comical way,
As shells become the turtles' play.
They wear them like hats upon their head,
Looking like they're ready for bed!

From sunrise to sunset they dance,
With wobbly shells that threaten a chance.
A flip and a flop, they joyfully swim,
With laughter that echoes along the brim.

Oh, the ocean's secrets they hold so dear,
In shells of time that bring such cheer.
Waddling home, they chuckle with glee,
"Did you see me? I'm as cool as can be!"

Driftwood Dreams

Driftwood swings like a rollercoaster,
Turtles ride it, not a single poster.
They giggle and jostle, as waves crash wide,
Catching all the joy down the ocean slide.

With each splash they try a new trick,
Balancing shells, it's quite the pick!
A turtle slips, let out a 'whoops!'
Convinced they'll join the jellyfish groups!

They dream of surfboards made of seaweed,
Sailing the tide, oh, what a speed!
But all they have is a soggy old log,
Yet turtle friends hop on like a fog!

So cheers to dreams in the salty spray,
Where laughter echoes both night and day.
With driftwood visions they splash and swirl,
Living the life, oh what a whirl!

The Silent Navigators

Underwater, they glide like kings,
With silent moves and flippy flings.
No need for maps or GPS calls,
Just bubbles for laughs and a few belly rolls.

With flippers wide, they make some waves,
In schools of fish, they're the comical knaves.
"Stop tickling me!" one joyful calls,
As crabs play tag along the coral walls.

Their eyes twinkle with mischief and fun,
As they chase the sun that's just begun.
Mistaking a buoy for a disco ball,
They dance and twirl, having a ball!

Silent navigators on laughter's spree,
With salty hair and a carefree glee.
In the great blue ocean, they're all the rage,
Writing their own funny sea page!

Tides of Transformation

With each wave that washes ashore,
The turtles giggle, ask for more!
Transforming shells like funny hats,
Becoming comedians, imagine that!

As tide rolls in, the show begins,
Turtle tummies full of tiny fins.
Slipping and sliding, what a scene,
"Watch out for my flip!" one turtle preens.

With every tide, they learn to dance,
Wiggling their tails in a serious prance.
Crabs clapping along, it's a jolly spree,
All in tune with their turtle glee!

So when the sun sets, and stars appear,
The turtles tell tales that we all cheer.
Transformations caught in seaside song,
In waves of laughter, they all belong!

Binding Ties to the Sea

In the sun, they paddle wide,
With shells that make them chubby and glide.
They wiggle their flippers, oh what a sight,
In a dance-off with fish, they take flight.

But wait, what's that? A plastic bag?
A turtle's dinner? Oh, that's just a drag!
They try to munch, but it's just a tease,
"Gourmet seafood? Please!" they say with a wheeze.

A group of pals in a turtle race,
One trips on coral, what a slow-paced chase!
With laughter echoing in the ocean blue,
"I swear I can win, it's just my shoe!"

The waves wash secrets under the foam,
Turtles gather to plan their home.
With a flip and a flop they set their fate,
"I told you not to eat the seaweed plate!"

A Lightweight Heart

With hearts so light, they ride the tide,
In search of jellybeans, they cannot hide.
Flippers flapping like silly flags,
Chasing bubbles and seaweed rags.

"Hey, Timmy, do you know how to dive?"
"Yes, but I might not survive!"
They tumble and twist, land in a swirl,
A whirlpool of giggles begins to unfurl.

They wear their shells like party hats,
"Don't forget to smile," says a turtle named Pat!
In a bubble of laughter, they float with glee,
Fins waving wildly, just wait and see!

The ocean blooms with their sparkly cheer,
"Who needs a map? The fun's right here!"
They bounce along through coral veils,
Turtles and jokes, with sea-foam trails.

The Flowing Ballet

In the water, a graceful ballet,
With swirls and twirls, they steal the day.
Turtles prance like ballet pros,
Spinning round like wiggly foes.

But who tripped over a sea sponge?
"Oops, my bad," they say with a lunge!
Laughter erupts from the deep blue sea,
As they shuffle and slide with undying glee.

A giant wave crashes, the music swells,
Turtles laugh and tell their jokes and spells.
"Now that's a splash! Can you feel that flow?"
"More like a belly flop!" as everyone glows.

With a wink and a flip, they take a bow,
"A round of applause, for the turtles now!"
They leap, they dance, they swim away bright,
In a flowing ballet beneath moonlight.

Feathered Waters

In feathered waters, where turtles roam,
They don on seaweed, making it home.
With style and flair, they strut their stuff,
"Who knew the ocean could be so tough?"

They chatter and chuckle, shells shining bright,
Chasing crabs that run with all their might.
"Catch me if you can," a crab shouts bold,
But turtle, with grace, just won't be sold.

In a race with waves that bubble and roll,
Turtles dash like they've found their whole soul.
"I need a snack, do we have some fries?"
"I'm on a seafood diet!" one turtle replies.

So as they splash under the sun's gleam,
Their giggles echo, a beautiful dream.
With friends all around, there's no place to flee,
In feathered waters, they're wild and free!

Sheltered by the Tide

A turtle in a shell so round,
Waddles on the sandy ground.
"Watch my moves!" she starts to dance,
While crabs appear and steal her chance.

She slips and slides, a goofy sight,
Doing somersaults, what pure delight!
"Hey, slow down!" her buddy yells,
As jellyfish toss their spiky gels.

The sun beats down, oh what a spree,
They build a castle by the sea.
With driftwood walls and shells so neat,
Turtles relax, life's such a treat!

But when it's lunch, oh what a chase,
As seaweed flies all over the place.
With snacks in tow, they giggle and grin,
"Next round's on me!" Let the fun begin!

Retreat of the Sea Spirits

Beneath the waves, where spirits play,
Turtles sing and dance all day.
To their tunes, all fishes sway,
Feeling groovy in a fishy way.

A turtle twirls with a splashy spin,
"Join our dance!" their friend yells in.
Crabs clap claws, oh what a scene,
While octopuses act like a queen.

They play peek-a-boo with a swift dolphin,
Catching waves like it's a sin.
"Sorry, fishy! I'm not your bait!"
As they ride the crest, feeling great!

"Let's take a break!" an elder shouts,
From chasing waves and sprightly bouts.
Together, they munch on seaweed wraps,
While washing down with algae taps!

The Call of the Wave Riders

On board a wave, the turtles glide,
With surfboards made of driftwood pride.
"Catch this wave!" the leader shouts,
While seagulls squawk, creating clouts.

They tumble down, a splashy scene,
As they balance, a wobbly routine.
"Hang ten!" the bravest turtle cries,
While belly flops earn surprise sighs.

The wind is wild, a joyful rush,
As turtles huddle, ready to crush.
With waves so tall, they shriek and cheer,
"We're the kings of surf! Let's grab a beer!"

But rogue waves come, excitement swells,
As sea stars dance with all their bells.
End the day with tales so bold,
Of daring rides that never grow old!

Currents of Time and Tides

In the deep blue, currents swirl,
Turtles twirl like a woolly curl.
"Catch that tide!" one shouts with gleam,
As fishes giggle, living the dream.

They race along, a comical bunch,
With tumbles and flops, it's quite the punch.
"Whoa, slow down!" old Timer barks,
As turtles whirl through coral parks.

When dusk retreats, with stars above,
They gather 'round for tales of love.
"Remember that time we swam too fast?"
"And ended up stuck in a jelly's grasp!"

With laughter bright, they make a toast,
To salty waves and life's great coast.
In bubbly tides, with spirits bold,
They weave their tales, forever told.

Shadows Beneath the Surface

In the ocean's depths, they poke and glide,
With flippers flapping, they take us for a ride.
Turtles in sunglasses, looking quite cool,
Chasing jellyfish like a playful fool.

They float through the kelp, munching on grass,
Thinking of dinner as the hours pass.
One turtle quips, 'What's on the menu tonight?'
'How about some plankton? It's a real delight!'

Friends with the fish, they share a wild chat,
Listening to dolphins gossip and chat.
'The wave was so big, I thought I'd get tossed!'
'You'd just do a flip—look, you're never lost!'

So here's to the turtles, cruising with flair,
A party under waves, without a care.
With bright shells and dreams swimming far and wide,
Together they frolic, on an oceanic ride.

Dance of the Sea Spirits

Beneath the blue, where the bubbles go pop,
Turtles twist and twirl, they never want to stop.
In seaweed skirts, they shimmy in style,
Performing for fish, with laughter and a smile.

One turtle tripped, oh what a sight!
He spun like a top, then grinned with delight.
'Thought I was graceful, but look at me now,'
He waved to his pals, 'Let's take a bow!'

Jellyfish joined in, swaying with the beat,
Creating a rave with some jellyfish treat.
'Why do we party? Just look at the view!'
'And snacks are fantastic—have you tried the goo?'

Each splash and each ripple is a call to groove,
Beneath the moonlight, they make their move.
With laughter and cheer, they dance all night long,
In the magical sea, they all belong.

Voyage of the Gentle Giants

With shells like shields, they set out to roam,
Big-hearted turtles feel right at home.
Riding the current, with a silly grin,
'Just trying to figure out where to begin!'

Navigating waves like it's a road map,
'Excuse me, Mr. Fish, do you have a cap?'
The fish just giggled, 'You're quite lost today,'
'Follow my fin—there's a beach party, hooray!'

Plodding along, they search for some fun,
They play peek-a-boo with the glowing sun.
'See my new shell? It's radiant and bright!'
'Nice one!' they all laugh, 'Let's have a bite!'

From coral to coast, they explore new lands,
Adventures unfold in the soft, silty sands.
With laughter and joy, they conquer the seas,
A crew of warm turtles, forever at ease.

Rippled Stories

In the depths below, ripples swirl with glee,
Turtles weaving tales as free as can be.
'Have you heard the one about the sandbar dance?'
'It was quite the party, what a wild chance!'

Each wave brings a giggle, a splash, then a tale,
'The time I got tangled in some seaweed hail.'
A turtle exclaimed with a chuckle so loud,
'Thought I was a mermaid—would've made you proud!'

Tales of the ocean spread quicker than light,
From turtles to sharks, they share deep delight.
With laughter echoing from the coral caves,
Stories collide like the fun-loving waves.

And as the sun sets with hues rich and warm,
The turtles gather close, sheltered from harm.
With hearts full of laughter and fins intertwined,
Their stories ripple on, forever enshrined.

Celestial Navigators

With shells like a car's, they zoom in the bay,
Finding their way, come what may!
In hats made of seaweed, they laugh and they roam,
Mapping the ocean, they're far from their home.

They dodge all the currents, they wiggle and twist,
Performing a dance, they can't resist!
On seashell surfboards, they ride with such grace,
These turtles are stars in the salty wet race.

The sun is their compass, the tides do their thing,
A party in waves, where the sea critters sing.
From reefs to the corals, they shimmy and dive,
Each turtle a scholar, they're wild and alive!

So if you see them, give a cheerful cheer,
For these quirky creatures bring oceans near!
The globetrotter turtles, with joy in their hearts,
Are silly sea heroes in watery arts.

Serpentines of the Sea

Through gardens of kelp, they slither and slide,
  Wiggly and wobbly, with nothing to hide.
They crack up the fish with their goofy parade,
  Sashaying through bubbles, adventure is made.

Sea urchins giggle as they scoot on their way,
These turtles are jokers, come join in the play!
With oceanic laughter, they surf every swell,
  In costumes of barnacles, they wriggle so well.

When dolphins come dancing, they join in the fun,
  Splashing and twirling 'til the day is all done.
With sea stars as witness, and crabs on the band,
  These turtles remind us, let joy be your wand!

So when you see them in a sparkling spree,
  Remember the fun in the expanse of the sea!
With flippers like ribbons, they twirl in delight,
Serpentines of laughter in the moon's shining light.

Beneath the Silver Moon

At night, when the moon casts a curious glow,
Turtles make plans in the tide's gentle flow.
With mischief in mind and a laugh in their wake,
They waddle and paddle, make no mistake!

Under the starlight, they play hide and seek,
With squids dressing up in a costume peak.
These turtles just giggle, peeking from shells,
In a world full of laughter, where no one compels.

Like clumsy old dancers, they flop through the sea,
Each splash is a story, so wild and so free!
They steal all the snacks from the fish on the run,
And swap them for jokes, oh what silly fun!

So when shadows stir in the water's embrace,
With chuckles they dance, giving joy a new face.
Beneath the silver moon, let your spirit take flight,
With turtles as friends, every moment's delight!

Odysseys of the Deep Blue

In quests of the deep, where the seaweed does sway,
Turtles embark on a whimsical way.
With goggles and flippers, they swim with a grin,
Exploring the wonders that lie deep within.

They leap over jellyfish, land with a flop,
Chasing down seahorses, never will stop!
With antics so bright, they turn day into night,
Tales woven of bubbles, in frolics they write.

Each wave is a riddle, each ripple a joke,
In the laughter of corals, their joy will provoke.
Through shipwrecks and treasures, they wander with glee,

Sharing stories of fun with the bright algae sea.

So join in the fun, let your spirit set free,
With turtles who'll make you as silly as can be!
Odysseys flowing in the ocean so wide,
With laughter and joy, they take all in stride.

www.ingramcontent.com/pod-product-compliance
Lightning Source LLC
Chambersburg PA
CBHW060139230426
43661CB00003B/486